Creeds of Faith
and
Inspiration

Blue Mountain Press ®

Boulder, Colorado

Creeds of Faith and Inspiration

A collection of poems
Edited by Robin Andrews

Library of Congress Catalog Card Number: 90-83142
ISBN: 0-88396-283-7

ACKNOWLEDGMENTS appear on page 62.

∎ design on book cover is registered in
U.S. Patent and Trademark Office.

Manufactured in the United States of America
First Printing: October, 1990

Blue Mountain Press ®

P.O. Box 4549, Boulder, Colorado 80306

CONTENTS

Anything Is Possible
Because of God

It is God who enables you
to smile in spite of tears;
to carry on when you feel like giving in;
to pray when you're at a loss for words;
to love even though your heart has been
  broken time and time again;
to sit calmly when you feel like throwing
  up your hands in frustration;
to be understanding when nothing
  seems to make sense;
to listen when you'd really rather not hear;
to share your feelings with others,
  because sharing is necessary
    to ease the load.

Anything is possible,
because God makes it so.

—Faye Sweeney

God Is Always There for You

In living this life,
you may find obstacles
   that cannot be surpassed,
and you may find problems that
   cannot be conquered alone.

Remember . . .
   while you're shouldering
the burdens and enduring the
trials and tribulations . . .
   you're never alone.

Even on the darkest nights,
you have a caring arm around you.
It is when all is dark that
  God's most loving light
    is shed into your soul.

You never walk alone.

God is always there
  to give you a reason
    to go on.

—Grace Lofton Taranto

Always Pray for the Best, and Live One Day at a Time

We cannot change the past;
we just need to keep
the good memories
and acquire wisdom
from the mistakes we've made.
We cannot predict the future;
we just need to hope and pray
for the best and what is right,
and believe that's how it will be.
We can live a day at a time,
enjoying the present
and always seeking to become
a more loving and better person.

—Karen Berry

There Is So Much to Be Thankful For

We don't often
take the time out of
our busy lives
to think about all
the beautiful things
and to be thankful for them
If we did
reflect on these things
we would realize how very
lucky and fortunate we really are

I am very thankful
for the love of my husband —
which is so complete and fulfilling
and is based on honesty, equality
intellectualism and romance

I am very thankful
for the love of my children —
which is all encompassing
and is based on teaching, tenderness
sensitivity, caring and hugging

I am very thankful
that I am able to love
and that the love is returned to me

I am very thankful
that I am healthy
and that the people I love
are healthy

I am very thankful
that I have dreams to follow
and goals to strive for

I am very thankful
for the beauty of nature —
magnificent mountains
the colorful leaves
the smell of the flowers
the roaring of the waves
the setting sun
the rising moon

Everywhere I look
I see the wonders of nature
and I feel so proud
to be a small part of it

I am very thankful
for all the good people in the world
I am very thankful
that I have good friends

I am very thankful
to be alive
in a time when
we can make the world
a better place
to live in

—Susan Polis Schutz

The Serenity Prayer

God grant me the serenity
to accept the things
    I cannot change;
the courage to change
    the things I can;
and the wisdom
    to know the difference.

—Reinhold Niebuhr

You Can Always
Look to God

If the day ahead
seems to be full of trouble,
and there are too many things
that you don't understand,
look to God.
He will show you there is
no trouble or confusion
that He cannot help you overcome.
He will be your comfort
through every storm
and surround you with His love
when you are feeling most alone.

If you feel so confused
that you're not sure
you'll ever be able
to straighten things out,
look to God.
He will calm your mind
and ease your fears.
He will strengthen
your faith and courage,
and He will help you
hold on until tomorrow
when the day ahead
will dawn with new hope
and promises of happiness.

—Donna Levine

A Blessing Asked
Especially for You

I pray that
God will guide you
in your decisions;
that He will quiet you
amid the world's confusion;
and that He will comfort you
  and carry you
over the times when you feel
that you cannot make it alone.

And I pray that He will
always let me be
there beside you
to let you know. . .

that wherever
  our hearts may be,
you may feel safe
  and loved
    and at home.

— Collin McCarty

God's Peace Is Always with You

"Don't worry about anything. Instead, pray about everything.

Tell God your needs...
His peace will keep your thoughts and your heart at peace."

— Philippians 4:6-7

God's Blessings
Are Ours to Cherish

There is so much to be thankful for
    in this world —
the love of our family,
a warm home, good friends,
our health and happiness,
the beauty that surrounds us.

Yet when things aren't going our way,
when sorrow enters our lives
or dreams seem out of reach,
we too quickly forget how fortunate
    we really are.

When difficulties occur,
we must learn to rise above the
feelings of sadness and despair.
We must accept the wisdom of God's plan
and go on with our lives,
grateful for His many blessings,
secure in His love.

—Anna Marie Edwards

"God Will Be There for You"

Some of the best advice
a person can share
   with someone they care about
      is this . . .

"God will be there for you."

If you need to lean on someone,
   there is no greater strength.
If you need to move away from
   difficulty and move towards resolve,
   there is no greater direction to go in.
If you wish to walk with happiness,
there is no greater travelling companion.

   Follow your heart when it tells you
   to believe, because there is no end
         to the blessings
            you can receive.

      "God will be there
         for you."

—Alin Austin

God grant me the strength
to reach out for my dreams
and see the world
with understanding and love,
and believe in the beauty
of life and the dignity of mankind.

—Andrew Harding Allen

What has happened
before in our lives
is all passed;
what we have been
and what we have done
belong to yesterday.

What we are
and what we can be —
with God's help —
is our today.

—Pauline Smith

This life is yours
Take the power
to choose what you want to do
and do it well
Take the power
to love what you want in life
and love it honestly
Take the power
to walk in the forest
and be a part of nature
Take the power
to control your own life
No one else can do it for you
Take the power
to make your life
healthy
exciting
worthwhile
and very happy

—Susan Polis Schutz

You Can Be Perfect in God's Eyes by Living Your Life with Love

Perfection is not gained
by doing some great thing well,
but by doing well
the simple tasks of life.
Perfection is not gained
by thinking some great truth,
but by living the simplicity of Truth
in daily life.

Everything which will ever come
into your life
affords you the opportunity to see
and be perfection.
Even the most simple task,
done with humility and love,
can be performed as a gift to your God.

Don't wait to be perfect.
You are perfect when you live your life
as love in action.
May the perfection which is God
be expressed by you today.

—W. Norman Cooper

Faith is to believe what we do not see; and the reward of this faith is to see what we believe.

—St. Augustine

Ask and it shall be given you;
seek and ye shall find;
knock and it shall be opened unto you.

—Matthew 7:7

You Can Do Anything
if You Believe

You can do anything if you believe.
If you take God's hand,
   then you will receive.
Pure peace and calm
   and love He will supply —
courage and patience
   you cannot deny.
See yourself perfect and whole
   every day;
      don't let the negatives
         stand in your way.

With the faith of a child,
   you can honestly know
the opportunity is yours
   to strengthen and grow.
Believe every second
   that you always have hope,
strength to endure,
      and ability to cope.
But far beyond this,
   you'll find peace of mind;
if you trust in the Lord,
   the answers you'll find.
Believe you can do anything;
   let it always be true,
and the best things in life
   will be open to you.

—Edna Louise

May God bless you with good health and close friends every day the whole year through. May God protect you and look after the loved ones around you. May God love you and always be near, wherever you go.

—Arida Fuller

There is hardly ever a complete silence in our soul.
God is whispering to us well-nigh incessantly.
Whenever the sounds of the world die out in the
soul, or sink low, then we hear these whisperings of
God. He is always whispering to us, only we do
not always hear, because of the noise, hurry, and
distraction which life causes as it rushes on.

— Faber

To be capable of knowing God, and to wish and hope to know him, is the road which leads straight to the Good; and it is an easy road to travel. Everywhere God will come to meet you, everywhere He will appear to you, at places and times at which you look not for it, in your waking hours and in your sleep, when you are journeying by water and by land, in the nighttime and in the daytime, when you are speaking and when you are silent; for there is nothing which is not God.

— Hermes

Prayer is so simple.
It is like quietly opening a door
And slipping into
The very presence of God.
There, in the stillness,
To listen for His voice,
Perhaps in petition
Or only to listen,
It matters not.
Just to be there,
In His presence,
Is prayer.

—Anonymous

More things are wrought by prayer
Than this world dreams of.

—Alfred, Lord Tennyson

God Is in Our Hearts
to See Us Through Each Day

No matter what your needs may be
you can depend upon
the divine Power within
to uplift, to bless,
and to strengthen you,
so that you in turn may uplift,
bless, and strengthen others.
You can depend upon this Power
to give you courage to meet with poise,
confidence, and peace of mind
each situation which this day
may present.

—W. Norman Cooper

May I seek to live this day
quietly, easily,
leaning on God's mighty strength
trustfully, restfully,
meeting others in the path
peacefully, joyously,
waiting for God's will unfolding
patiently, serenely,
facing what tomorrow brings
confidently, courageously.

—Anonymous

From Whence Shall My Help Come?

"I will lift up my eyes to the mountains;
From whence shall my help come?
My help comes from the Lord,
Who made heaven and earth.
He will not allow your foot to slip;
He who keeps you will not slumber . . .

The Lord is your keeper;
The Lord is your shade on your right hand.
The sun will not smite you by day,
Nor the moon by night.
The Lord will protect you from all evil;
He will keep your soul.
The Lord will guard your going out
    and your coming in
From this time forth and forever."

—Psalm 121

Hold fast to your faith in God.
You're not being promised
days filled with sunshine
or no pain,
but in Him you'll find some peace
to get through each day.
Questions will always come to mind . . .
Why me?
What did I do wrong?

It is good to search for the answers,
but admit your mistakes
and get on with life.
It's not easy,
so take one day at a time.
Brighter days will come;
it's just a matter of time.
You're not alone;
there are many who feel as you do.
It's just your faith that
will pull you through.

—Sherrie L. Householder

I know that lately you
have been having problems
and I just want you to know
that you can rely on me
   for anything
you might need
But more important
keep in mind at all times
that you are very capable
of dealing with any complications
that life has to offer
So
do whatever you must
feel whatever you must
and keep in mind at all times
that we all
grow wiser and
become more sensitive and
are able to enjoy life more
after we go through
hard times

—Susan Polis Schutz

To every thing there is a season, and a time
to every purpose under heaven;

A time to be born, and a time to die; a
time to plant, and a time to pluck up
that which is planted;

A time to kill, and a time to heal; a time
to break down, and a time to build up;

A time to weep, and a time to laugh; a
time to mourn, and a time to dance;

A time to cast away stones, and a time
to gather stones together; a time to embrace,
and a time to refrain from embracing;

A time to get, and a time to lose; a time
to keep, and a time to cast away;

A time to rend, and a time to sew; a time
to keep silence, and a time to speak;

A time to love, and a time to hate; a
time of war, and a time of peace.

— Ecclesiastes 3:1-8

Lord, make me an
  instrument of your peace.
Where there is hatred,
let me sow love;
where there is injury, pardon;
where there is doubt, faith;
where there is despair, hope;
where there is darkness, light;
and where there is sadness, joy.

—St. Francis of Assisi

We need to feel more
to understand others
We need to love more
to be loved back
We need to cry more
to cleanse ourselves
We need to laugh more
to enjoy ourselves

We need to establish the values
    of honesty and fairness
when interacting with people
We need to establish
    a strong ethical basis
as a way of life

We need to see more
other than our own little fantasies
We need to hear more
and listen to the needs of others

We need to give more
and take less
We need to share more
and own less
We need to realize
    the importance of the family
as a backbone to stability
We need to look more
and realize that we are not
    so different from one another

We need to create a world where
we can all peacefully live
the life we choose
We need to create a world where
we can trust each other

                    —Susan Polis Schutz

Let God Help

He has helped so many through
so much.
And He will be there for you
in your most personal moments
and through the times of your life,
whether they are troubled
or triumphant.

Take comfort in that thought.
And hold it inside you
this day and all the days
of your life.

—Alin Austin

God Is Always with You

When we are in the middle
of a difficult time,
we need to remember that
we can rely on God for strength,
inspiration, and guidance.
We never need to be alone
for He will always be with us,
if we seek Him.
His protection and healing
are ours for the asking,
and His will for us
is for our health and happiness.

There is no sadness that
God cannot help us through,
no pain that He cannot
change to well-being,
no loss that He cannot
help us recover from,
and no trouble that He
cannot turn to gladness.

—Donna Levine

Faith Is What
Gives Life Meaning

Living life on the faith-only basis is what makes life worth living. It gives life its meaning. . . . Faith is leaping across gaps that exist between the known and the unknown; the proven and the unproven; the actual and the possible; the grasp and the reach; the "I've got it" and "I want it"; the knowledge and the mystery; life and death; time and eternity.

Faith is making decisions before you've solved all the problems.

Faith is making commitments before you can be assured that everything will work out.

Faith is moving ahead before you have answers to all the questions.

Faith is taking a risk without being fully insured.

Faith is choosing to believe before there is total proof.

—Robert H. Schuller

Every Day, Let Us Be Thankful for God's Love

Every day is
a day to thank God
for all the blessings
He has given you.

Every day is
a day to ask God
to guide you with love
through the coming year
and thank Him
for standing by you
during the past one.

Every day
is a day to be grateful
for all the wonderful things
He has still to give you,
and for His help
in making you the person
you have always wanted to be.

—Donna Levine

ACKNOWLEDGMENTS

The following is a partial list of authors, publishers, and authors' representatives whom the publisher especially wishes to thank for permission to reprint their works.

Grace Lofton Taranto for "God Is Always There for You." Copyright © 1990 by Grace Lofton Taranto. All rights reserved. Reprinted by permission.

Donna Levine for "You Can Always Look to God," "God Is Always with You," and "Every Day, Let Us Be Thankful . . . ." Copyright © 1990 by Donna Levine. All rights reserved. Reprinted by permission.

Pauline Smith for "What has happened before . . . ." Copyright © 1990 by Pauline Smith. All rights reserved. Reprinted by permission.

W. Norman Cooper for "You Can Be Perfect in God's Eyes . . ." and "God Is in Our Hearts . . . ." From **Seize the Day**, by W. Norman Cooper. Copyright © 1986 by Truth Center. All rights reserved. Reprinted by permission.

Edna Louise for "You Can Do Anything if You Believe." Copyright © 1984 by Edna Louise. All rights reserved. Reprinted by permission.

Sherrie L. Householder for "Hold fast to your faith in God." Copyright © 1990 by Sherrie L. Householder. All rights reserved. Reprinted by permission.

Thomas Nelson, Inc. for "Faith Is What Gives Life Meaning," by Robert H. Schuller. From **Be Happy, You Are Loved**, by Robert H. Schuller. Copyright © 1986 by Robert H. Schuller. All rights reserved. Reprinted by permission.

A careful effort has been made to trace the ownership of poems used in this anthology in order to obtain permission to reprint copyrighted materials and to give proper credit to the copyright owners. If any error or omission has occurred, it is completely inadvertent, and we would like to make corrections in future editions provided that written notification is made to the publisher:

BLUE MOUNTAIN PRESS, INC., P.O. Box 4549, Boulder, Colorado 80306.